We hadn't driven very far when the truck stopped, and I heard Peter greet Dr. Torok. The door closed and we were off on our escape from Hungary.

We drove through Aszad and Vac. A few miles beyond Vac I noticed a thumping noise. I banged on the cab to get Istvan's attention, and he pulled over to the side of the road. Istvan got out and came around the truck.

"We've got a flat tire!" He announced.

"Dr. Torok, climb into the back while Peter and I change the tire," Istvan continued.

While they were changing the tire a truck pulled up, and two German soldiers got out and asked, "What's the problem?"

"We have a flat tire. We would appreciate your helping us fix it," Istvan answered back.

Since there was work involved, they immediately climbed back into their truck and left. Peter and Istvan returned to changing the tire, and soon we were on our way to Szob.

AL FEHER

Escape From Hungary

by
Al Feher

Westview Publishing Co., Inc., Nashville, Tennessee

This book is a work of fiction.

First Edition published 2005

Printed in the United States of America on acid-free paper

ISBN 0-9773179-0-0

Acquisitions Editor – Hugh Daniel
Layout and other pre-press by
    Westview Publishing Co., Inc.

Westview Publishing Co., Inc.
8120 Sawyer Brown Road, Suite 107
PO Box 210183
Nashville, TN 37221
westviewpublishing.com

Contents

AL FEHER

Illustrations

CHAPTER ONE

Ground to Air to Ground

I awoke to the clanking of tanks racing past my foxhole. It sounded like the surf of the Atlantic Ocean off Fire Island, Long Island, N.Y.

"Gosh, I wish I were back there," I thought.

George Agardi and I rode our bicycles to Sayville from Ronkonkoma and then took the ferryboat to Fire Island. We would camp out in the dunes for a few days and cook our meals over a fire made of driftwood. My Uncle Gene taught me how to roast ears of corn when he took me to Fire Island. We tied the ends of the husks, dug a hole, placed the corn in the hole, and covered it with sand. We would then build a fire over the corn and allow it to cook. When it was finished, it was sweet and very tasteful.

When we were ready to return on the ferry, George and I realized that we didn't have enough money for the fare. We had to go back to the shoreline and hunt for one-gallon glass jugs, which we turned in for a five-cent deposit on each bottle. When we had enough money, we returned to the ferry and paid our fare to Sayville.

Who would have thought back then that soon many other teen-aged Americans and I would be taking a much larger boat, the Queen Mary, to another island.

Sometimes I wondered how the allies won the war.

I remember an incident when we moved quite a few

miles forward. When we arrived at a small forest of trees we were told to dig a foxhole and spent the night. I thought I knew better and decided to sleep on the seat of a bulldozer. During the night I awoke from the noise of several tanks going by within three hundred yards of us. Fifteen or twenty minutes later another group of tanks came by and happened to see the light of one sentry's cigarette. They stopped and soon were on their way. Later the sentry told us the first group was German tanks and the second group was Americans. The Americans, part of Patton's Third Army had been chasing the Germans for hours. Our captain told us to pack up and we turned around and drove a half hour and stopped in a similar forest as last night. Later we found out that Captain Graves had read his map wrong.

Upon my induction into the Army, I was shipped to Camp Upton in Yaphank, New York for processing. In a few days I was on a train for Camp Butner, North Carolina and assigned to Headquarters Co., 311th Battalion, 78th Infantry Division. Here at Butner I took 16 weeks of basic training.

Following basic training I read where the Air Force was taking recruits for Air Cadet training provided they could pass the physical and mental tests. What better way to get out of the Infantry! I applied, took the tests and passed. Soon I received my orders to report to Keesler Field in Biloxi, Mississippi.

There I took my physical and psycomotive tests and passed with flying colors. Who would have thought that a high school graduate would soon be training to become a pilot?

Just before Thanksgiving, we boarded a train for Burlington, Vermont to begin our training. We traveled by Pullman, two to a compartment with separate beds and private bathroom facilities and all the comforts of home.

We arrived in Burlington with snow on the ground and unloaded our duffel bags and began the climb up a steep hill to the University of Vermont. Soon we were shedding our coats and jackets because of the hard work climbing.

We took classes in weather, math, science and other related courses that would assist us in the flight program. We were issued a flight jacket and log book and assigned an instructor to begin our ten hours of pre-flight. Thank God for Lake Champlain, as you could not get lost if you kept the lake in sight!

I enjoyed my stay in Burlington and even tried to ski on our off days. Sundays we took horse drawn sleighs to the outskirts of Burlington where the members of a local church treated us to a delicious dinner.

One day we were asked to assemble where we were given a copy of General "Hap" Arnold's letter stating that we were to return to the ground forces (page 24-B). This was because of the shortage that developed since the last selective service and these fine American soldiers who will want to do the greatest damage to the enemy. I preferred to this damage from the air.

We packed and boarded a troop train for Camp Picket, Virginia but this time we traveled by coach, two men per seat, and ate from our mess kits in a chow line. How soon they can put you back in your place! Two days later I was back in the same outfit that I had left, the 311th Battalion, 78th Infantry Division. We were put on KP every weekend for three weeks straight and complained loud and clear.

Again we were told to be ready and packed as we were going back to the Air Force in the morning. Naturally we couldn't sleep that night and awoke earlier than usual.

They loaded us in two and half-ton trucks and we were soon off on our way to the Air Force. We hadn't driven a mile or so when the trucks stopped and we were told to get off. I looked around and couldn't see an airfield or any planes. All I could see was row on row of wooden barracks, our home for several months. We were welcomed to Company A 264th Combat Engineers where we would be taught how to construct wooden bridges and pontoon bridges.

Following that training we left for overseas and soon landed in Scotland and then rode a train to Crewe, England. There we were shown to our barracks. I went to the latrine, brushed my teeth, and shaved what few facial hairs I had. Damn! The water was cold there. Lucky for me that I only had to shave once every two weeks.

We would be in Crewe long enough to receive training on how to build the 'Bailey Bridge', and shown how to recognize German weapons, land mines, and uniforms. After we finished erecting the bridge we went back to the bivouac area and had some well-deserved hot chow. Soon we turned in for the night.

Following the few weeks of training, we shipped out of Southampton for Le Harve, France.

Upon arriving in France we were issued ammunition for our weapons. We were then transported in two and a half ton trucks to our destination, which was Mannheim.

As we passed through France, all around us, we could see the aftermath of the Allied Armies pushing toward Berlin.

In Mannheim we unloaded the equipment and materials from the truck to the area where we were to construct a pontoon bridge over a small river.

CHAPTER TWO
Special Assignment

Corporal Buffman came over to where I was standing and told me that Captain Graves wanted to see me. I hoped that he didn't want me to take him back in the company jeep to see his old buddy from Texas A & M. The last trip that I took Captain Graves on was to see his college roommate I almost drove off a bombed out bridge and I caught hell when I turned on the headlights so that I could see to cross the pontoon bridge.

"What does he want?" I asked Buffman. Buffman was from Buffalo, New York and was our radioman and German interpreter.

"I don't know. I'm only carrying out orders," he answered.

Buffman and I found three cases of cognac while on patrol in a bombed out railroad station. We hid two cases and divided the other between First Sergeant Misiorek and Sergeant Mollihan. Buffman and I hoped it would help us later as we were doing a little brown nosing.

I finished what I was doing and walked over to Captain Graves' tent.

"Corporal Feher reporting sir," I said without saluting. (We had been told not to salute officers as snipers could shoot them.)

"I have your orders here. You are to report to General Meade's Headquarters at 0600 today. Pack all your belongings and be ready in an hour"

I asked, "Why am I going, where are his headquarters, and how am I going to get there?"

"No, I don't know why, but Sgt. Kelly will take you in a company jeep." "Good luck!" Captain Graves replied.

I packed my few belongings, said goodbye to a couple of friends and headed over to the jeep where Kelly was waiting. Kelly was from Salem, Virginia and we had spent some time together in Blackstone.

"What's going on?" I asked him. He answered, "All I know is that I am supposed to drive you to General Meade's Headquarters, and you are to report to Captain Adams."

As we were riding back to General Meade's headquarters, Kelly and I talked about the good times we had in Virginia. An hour later we were there.

I asked, "Where is his office?" Kelly pointed it out to me.

Captain Adams shifted in his chair and gazed at me as though I knew why I was asked to be there.

"At this moment our conversation is being taped. It's your right to know that, he retorted. "You must swear to secrecy the information given to you, not only in the interest of national security, but in the future of the outcome of ending the war as soon as possible," he continued.

"How can I agree to something like that when I have

no idea what the information is and what you want me to do?" I asked.

"Because I can give you a quick idea and it'll be enough for you to say, yes or no. If it's no, you'll be escorted out of here and driven back to your outfit and no one will be the wiser," he answered.

"Go ahead," I replied.

"All right," Captain Adams spoke calmly.

When Captain Adams started to speak, the telephone rang and this gave me time to think of a hundred reasons for my being there or my leaving. I understood and spoke Hungarian reasonably well. I was a good swimmer, and I had ten hours of flight instruction before being assigned to the 264th Combat Engineers. That reminded me of the letter from Hap Arnold saying that all who had prior ground force experience wanted to get back and fight the enemy as soon as possible. It couldn't have been flying, as I wasn't proficient enough. What could he want of me?

Captain Adams finished his conversation, put down the phone, and again spoke calmly, "Feher I understand that both your parents were born in Hungary."

"Yes sir," I replied.

"I also see here in your records that you are a good swimmer and certified Red Cross Water Instructor."

Again I replied, "Yes Sir."

Adams asked me if I wanted him to continue, and I told him yes. I wondered what else they knew about me?

Adams continued, " There is a town in Hungary

called Hatvan."

I knew that Hatvan meant 60 and later learned that this town was 60 kilometers Northeast of Budapest.

The Captain said, "There is a factory there owned by the Krupp Family, and they manufacture various kinds of war materials, namely mortars, 88's shells and various weapons. Our people have learned that the factory is working on a jet engine for fighter planes and are harvesting atomic energy by splitting uranium atoms. The Krupp factory like many others is using forced labor, Jews, Gypsies, and anyone who has any training as an engineer whatever their nationality. There is a Hungarian engineer working at this factory named Sandor Torok. His family fled Hungary before the Germans occupied their country, and they have related to the British that he wants out of the country. He asked me if I wanted him to continue.

"Yes Sir," I answered as my thoughts were going elsewhere.

When I was young I recall my grandmother speaking to my parents and our relatives in Hungarian. As I grew older and could understand what they were saying, they spoke in German whenever they didn't want my sister or me to understand. My mother's maiden name was Sturman. She, along with two sisters and a brother, was born in Nagy Roze, a town north of Budapest. My father was born in Bekescsabab, which was in the eastern part of Hungary close to Romania. My parents met in New York, Astoria, where my grandmother owned a bakery store. My grandfather, John Sturman died before I was born and he wanted to be cremated and buried in Hungary. My grandmother and mother returned to Hungary, and his ashes were buried in his Nagy Roze. My mother was fifteen years old when she arrived at Ellis Island in 1913.

After World War I the town was renamed Revuca and is now a part of Slovakia. My daughters and I visited Revuca in 1996 to look for my grandfather's grave. We couldn't find it as that part of the cemetery was all grown up. We did find the name Von Terpersers on many grave markers. This was my grandmother's maiden name. I want to return and find my grandfather's burial site.

Captain Adams continued, "Your objective is to meet with Torok and convince him to leave Hungary. You are to escort him to the landing point near Esztergom where you will signal for your return."

"Upon arriving in Hungary you will meet with two Hungarians who are loyal to the Allies and who detest Germans and Russians. You are to make your way to Budapest and make contact at the Matthias Church on the Buda side of the Danube River. Each night at 6:00 p.m. you are to wait until contact is made. I will be holding a copy of the MAGYAR ORSOG newspaper. Your contact will confront you and say, "What awful weather!" (*Micsoda pocsek ido van!*) You are to answer, "Isn't it cold?" (*Nincs hideg?*) Then you are to tell them your name, and they will tell you theirs. You will then cross over the Danube River on the Margit Hid (Margaret Bridge) and proceed to the safe house on Garam Ut. (Garam Street) in Pest. You will wear civilian clothes over your uniform, and if needed take them off in a hurry.

Captain Adams lit a cigarette, and sat back and waited as I was being issued new gear.

Instead of a steel helmet, which I had been wearing for months, I was issued a soft overseas hat. I was also issued a honed knife and a .45 pistol, which I decided to leave behind. I kept a compass and flashlight.

CHAPTER THREE
Into Hungary

After a dress rehearsal, Captain Adams decided I was set. Now I was only waiting for it to get dark.

While waiting Sgt. Bill Silverman prepared a hot meal for me. The cooks looked as though they knew something was up and gave me a few pats on the back. After I washed my mess kit, Sgt. Silverman gave me four K-ration chocolate bars and four full K-rations and said, "When you come back to the Company, I'll have a good hot meal waiting for you."

I took off about 6:45 p.m. I rechecked my gear and jumped into a jeep. In a few minutes we were up to the area that I planned to cross. It was a few miles from Esztergom. We stopped and got out of the jeep. I began to wonder if the clothes I had on were enough to keep me warm. It was cold and had begun to snow. In a way I was glad it was snowing as I hoped the Germans would be inside keeping warm.

A few feet away I met the group who was to take me across. I got into the boat and they slid it into the water. It seemed it took hours to get across. I could hear the paddles in the water and was sure that we would be heard. Everything would be called off if that happened, but it didn't.

Previous arrangements were made for my return. I could signal them by flashlight when I came back. The password was "National" answered by "American" which were the names of the two baseball leagues.

They asked me when I thought I would be back and I told them within two weeks. I also asked them to be there every day at 7p.m. Just in case something happened. I reminded them to be very quiet when going back. After a few seconds I could no longer see them. I was now alone.

Suddenly a flare lit up the sky, and I fell flat on the ground. I cautiously looked around, but there wasn't a Kraut in sight.

The hair on my head felt as though it was rising on a mad dog's back. My skin felt prickly all over, and I had a vacant feeling in my gut.

When the flare died out, I got up and circled around to the right. Flares continued to go off. Each time a flare burned out I crept forward. In about a half an hour I had covered less than 300 yards. I then cut across some fields for about two miles, and I decided that I was far enough away to get on a paved road. I walked right down the middle of it.

Just ahead I heard the rumble of a horse drawn vehicle. I scrambled into the ditch along the side of the road and waited for it to pass. In a couple of minutes I was on the road again. Further on I checked my compass and started on to Esztergom.

I came to a small town and decided to go around it, as I could smell smoke from stinking German cigarettes. I was now about two-thirds of the way to my destination, Budapest, and some distance behind enemy lines. I had a good feeling that I would be able to talk my way out of any situation that might occur.

I had walked about five miles when I came across another paved road. This should take me on toward Budapest. As I came around a bend to my amazement I saw a German halftrack. My stomach was knotting slowly and tightly with overpowering fear. Not fear of death or injury, but the fear of failure.

Looking around I spotted a clothing store. I sneaked in without being seen. I looked at a jacket and kept my eyes on the halftrack until it left. I quietly left the store and continued my journey.

I picked up the main road to Esztergom and decided that I would walk until I could find a place to stay for the night. Just before the sun settled, I saw a barn in the distance. I decided to wait for the sun to go down, and then I would go and spend the night there in the barn.

When it was dark and everyone on the farm had retired for the night I made my way toward the barn. I skirted around the house and entered the barn through the back door. Making my way as quietly as possible, I climbed up to the hayloft and settled in for the night. I was restless throughout the night, falling asleep from being tired and waking up from being cold.

Around 5 a.m. I awoke and decided that I should be on my way before someone came to the barn and found me. Once again I was on my way toward Esztergom.

I was feeling really good about my journey since I hadn't had any problems so far. But my feelings soon changed as a truck almost ran over me.

The driver stopped and asked, "Are you going to Esztergom?" I answered, "Yes." He offered me a ride and I took it.

We arrived at my destination in an hour or so. I thanked him and began looking for the ferry. I found it on my own, as I didn't want to ask too many questions and be noticed. The ferry was leaving in ten minutes.

I paid the fare and climbed aboard. I went to the men's room and cleaned myself up as best I could.

In twenty minutes we were on the other side of the Danube. As I got off the ferry I saw a sign pointing towards Budapest and began walking. Shortly I came upon a road sign pointing toward Dorog and Piliscsaba, and I knew I was on the right road.

I was on the road another 10 or 15 minutes when a car came by. It stopped and the driver offered me a ride. I jumped in the car and was glad for the ride and scared at the same time. I soon found out that he was Hungarian and was the owner of a jewelry store in Pest. He had been visiting his parents on the outskirts of Esztergom.

He asked, "Where are you from?"

"I was born in Bekescsabab, my father's birthplace, but I've been living in Germany and attending Heidelberg University. I'm on my way to visit relatives in Buda," I answered.

After some small talk we arrived in Buda, and I asked him to let me off at the next street corner. Before I got out of the car, I noticed a café across the street and decided that I must get something to eat. I was tired of

K-rations. I got out and thanked the man for the ride. I entered the café, sat down, and ordered something from the menu. I was soon served and the food was good. Of course it wasn't as good as my Mother's food. I finished my meal, checked my watch it was 5:30 p.m. and paid my bill. I left the café and proceeded toward Matthias Church where I was to meet my two Hungarian guides. I arrived at the church and bought the Magyar Orsog newspaper from a vendor outside.

Only then did I realize that if they had been sold out and I couldn't locate a paper, I would have lost a whole day. I had to be holding that newspaper in my hand as a signal for my guides.

I was standing in front of the church reading the paper when two men walked by, turned and said, "What awful weather!"

I answered, "Isn't it cold?"

I told them my name and they told me theirs.

Istvan, the older one said, "Come with us."

I walked between them and we headed for the Margaret Bridge.

As we were walking through Buda toward the bridge that would take us across the Danube, I wondered if I could trust my two companions. So far they turned out to be all I expected, and as I was briefed before my journey. I had to trust them, after all my life and the outcome of my assignment depended on them.

We hadn't been walking too long when I spotted two German soldiers approaching us. I tried to remain as calm as possible so as not to draw their attention.

When they were within five feet of us they stopped. I was sure that they were going to ask us for our papers, but one of them took out a pack of cigarettes and lit one. I was happy to smell those stinking German cigarettes. We stepped aside and walked around them continuing on our way to the safe house.

Soon we were across the Margaret Bridge and in Pest. Now my guides took me to the house on Garam Street where I would spend the night and receive my final instructions. We walked approximately a half-mile and turned left on Garam Street. Then we walked up a flight of steps to house number 16. Peter, the younger of the two, rang the bell and waited for someone to allow us to enter.

In a few minutes an elderly lady opened the door and Peter said in Hungarian, "I'm here on business (*Hivatalosan vagyok itt*)."

"What kind of business are you in (*Mi a foglalkozasa*)?" the lady wanted to know.

"I am Peter. This is Istvan and Sandor."

"Come on in," she said.

The four of us proceeded to the back of the house into the kitchen.

"Have a seat and I will prepare a meal for you," she told us.

Istvan and Peter talked to her while she was preparing the food and I kept quiet, as I really didn't know how much she knew about my reason for being there. Later I learned that the least she knew the less we would have to worry about if she were caught harboring an American.

I was getting sleepy. I had eaten too much and the pressure on me was great.

So far my trust was in my two guides, and now an old lady who seemed oblivious of the three of us.

I truly trusted my two Hungarian friends, as they could have turned me in several times. The old woman, I didn't know. I knew I had to get some sleep and hoped that my friends would take turns staying awake, just in case someone came to the door, or the phone rang, or anything else out of the ordinary happened.

When our lady friend finished in the kitchen, she left the three of us alone. Istvan suggested that we get up at 6 a.m., eat breakfast, and leave for Hatvan at seven.

Since the roads and bridges would be busy with people going to work, he felt that we would have a better chance of not being questioned. A truck would be left in front of the house for us to drive to Hatvan.

I must have been dozing because Istvan put his hand on my shoulder, shook me and told me to follow him to the basement where we would sleep. I gladly followed him down the stairs into a small room hidden behind a wall of canned fruits and vegetables.

There were two small cots and a mattress on the floor. I immediately took one of the cots, undressed and lay down. While lying in bed my thoughts were about the last two days I spent since getting into the boat and crossing the river. I had less than twelve days to accomplish my mission.

CHAPTER FOUR
The Trip to Hatvan

I must have fallen asleep immediately because I awoke with Peter standing over me.

"Breakfast is ready and we will have to leave soon," he said.

I went upstairs and ate a typical European meal of fruit, cheese, rolls, meat and coffee. When the three of us finished, I went over to my hostess and thanked her for sharing her home with us. She didn't respond, so I felt she was glad to get rid of us.

My two guides and I left for Hatvan by truck. I asked, "How am I supposed to make contact with Dr. Torok?" This was my objective for the assignment.

Istvan, the younger one, said, "I have been following Dr. Torok and have
learned where he lives. We have rented an apartment in the same building."

"You are to slowly gain his friendship and eventually show him the letter from his wife and the pictures of his family. After you have gained his confidence, you will reveal to him who you are. You will explain to him that his family wants him to join them in England. Tell him you are to assist him in his escape from the Germans."

I was also to tell him that the Allies knew what the Germans were hoping to manufacture there in Hatvan.

The guides and I stopped at a small café and had coffee and apple strudel. While dining with my two new friends I wondered if I had made a mistake in undertaking this assignment. What if I were caught? I couldn't reveal the true reason as to why I was in Hungary. My parents had no idea where I was or why! Would I be treated as a spy or a prisoner of war? I could tell them I was AWOL (absent without leave), but would they believe me? Regardless, it may have been another mistake wearing my uniform under my civilian clothes.

"What if we are stopped by Germans and I am caught?" I asked Istvan.

"You'll not be caught," he replied.

"I sure hope you're right, but what if?"

"We'll cross that bridge when we get there," Istvan answered in a dry voice.

I suggested that I would tell them that I was AWOL. Peter asked me what reason I would give for deserting my company.

"I will tell them I left for a Hungarian girl who visited my parents prior to the outbreak of the war."

Istvan laughed and said, "Where will we find this girl?"

Peter spoke up, "I have a cousin, her name is Margit, and she lives outside Aszod with my aunt and uncle. I could say we stopped by for me to visit them. It is only a few kilometers out of the way. I could talk to my cousin and tell her we need her to accompany us to Hatvan. I may have to say that you are an American soldier, and that you have deserted the American Army. She is to say that she met you in America and wanted to be with you on our trip to Hatvan."

Istvan agreed that it might be plausible.

We finished our coffee and left for Aszod.

The traffic was beginning to thin out, and we were able to make good time. Our truck was fairly new, a diesel manufactured in Germany.

Soon we were on the outskirts of Aszod, and we pulled up to the farm of Peter's Uncle. We got out of the truck and walked toward the farmhouse. While we were walking I noticed the roof was made of straw. I wondered if it was waterproof.

As Peter was about to knock on the door, it opened. His aunt greeted him. After introductions, hugs, and kisses Peter asked, "Where is Uncle and Cousin?"

"They're out in the barn milking the cows," she answered.

We left her at the door and went toward the barn. I noticed ducks off to our right, and they reminded me of the duck farms on Long Island. There whenever you drove by the duck farms, that looked like fields of snow.

The three of us entered the barn, and were immediately hit by an aroma that was pleasant to ones' nose. There is something about the smell of hay, cows, and horses.

Peter called out to his Uncle Tibor. An elderly man came out of one of the stalls with a milk pail.

We were introduced to Uncle Tibor and he asked,

"What are you doing in Aszod?"

Peter answered, "We are on our way to Hatvan, and I wanted my friends to meet you and Auntie."

"Where is Cousin Margit?" Peter asked.

His uncle called out for his daughter, and she appeared with a milk pail. When I saw her I hoped she would accompany us, because she was very attractive. With some cleaning up and a change of clothes I thought that the Germans might believe my story about going AWOL to be with Margit.

Peter introduced Margit to Istvan and me. She asked, "What are you doing in Aszod?"

"We are on our way to Hatvan on a very important mission for the Hungarian Government against the Germans," he answered.

"What is your mission?" She asked.

Peter replied, "I don't know if I should tell you..."

Margit said, "You know I hate the Krauts!" cutting his answer short.

I wondered when and how Peter or Istvan would tell her who I was and why I was there. Soon four people and maybe her parents would know that I was an American in occupied Hungary.

My thoughts returned to my home on Long Island. We hadn't been invaded by a foreign nation since the British came over. In America I could go anywhere without showing my personal papers to authorities. I could go to any church I desired and vote for anyone I wanted. Here in this country you could be stopped anywhere at anytime.

There was a lake in my hometown and we could swim in the summer, and go boating and fishing. In the winter we could go sleigh riding, skating, and ice boating on the frozen lake. Would I be able to return to Ronkonkoma and rejoin my family and relatives and do those things again?

I also thought about the Liberty Hall that was built by many Hungarians in Ronkonkoma. They held their meetings there, and I would make a fire for them in the winter to warm up the building.

Every Labor Day weekend they held the popular Grape Festival. Each year they would hire a Gypsy band to play all of the old Hungarian songs. My sisters, cousins and I would dress up in Hungarian costumes and enter the Hall singing Hungarian songs. Our elders taught us the czardas, a Hungarian dance, and we tried our best to do it.

Ours was a close-knit family. Each year we would celebrate Christmas together with my grandmother, my parents, aunts, and uncles. They would take turns hosting the family to celebrate the annual holiday.

Aszod was similar to Eastern Long Island with potatoes, cabbage and duck farms. But would I ever see home again? That question should be answered in less than two weeks.

Margit turned to leave the room and said, "I'm going to clean up and change clothes."

We went into the kitchen and sat down to a table of homemade bread, chicken paprika, cheese, fruit and wine. While we were eating Istvan told Margit's father, Tibor, why we were going to Hatvan.

Istvan said, "I hope we can trust you with what we are divulging. We also need your daughter to go with us if she will. Sandor needs an alibi as to why he is in Hungary if we were to get stopped by the Germans. We want Margit to be the alibi.

Now five people knew who I was, and why I was in Hungary. How many more would be told? How many of these could we trust?

Just as we were finishing our meal Margit walked in. She was all dressed up and looked prettier than when I met her in the barn.

Her mother brought more food for Margit, and she sat down at the table with the four of us.

"What brings the three of you to Aszod?" she asked, directing her question to her cousin.

Peter knew that sooner or later she would have to be told why we were there, and with Istvan's nod of approval Peter spoke.

"Sandor is an American soldier whose parents were both born in Hungary. He was given orders by the Americans and was landed by boat near Esztergom under cover of darkness. He proceeded to Buda where Istvan and I made contact with him. We are taking him to Hatvan where an apartment has been rented. A Dr. Torok lives in the same building. He is a Hungarian Jew who is an engineer at the Krupp Factory.

The factory is manufacturing a secret war weapon, and Dr. Torok heads the project. Sandor is to make the

Doctor's acquaintance and eventually show him a letter and pictures of his family who are living in England. His family expresses their desire for him to leave Hungary with Sandor."

"What does all of this have to do with me?" Margit interrupted.

Peter continued, " In case we are stopped by the Germans, Sandor does not have the proper papers, and he could be treated as a spy. His excuse for being here, hopefully they will believe him, is that he met you several years ago and left his unit without permission to be with you. You are to say that this reason is true, and we were on our way to the Grape Festival in Hatvan."

Margit looked at her mother and father as if to ask, "What should I do?"

Her father spoke up saying, "You know how I hate the Germans. They took four of my prized horses and five of my best head of cattle. I will leave it up to you whether you want to help them or not."

Margit's mother nodded in agreement with her husband.

Margit immediately answered, "I will go with you to Hatvan. I will go to my room and pack my belongings."

"We will do our very best to take care of her, as she is part of my family," Peter said convincingly to his Aunt and Uncle.

"I will prepare some food for you to take to Hatvan with you. My daughter is a big eater and I am also sure the three of you will also enjoy what I prepare," stated her mother.

The six of us walked outside, said our goodbyes, and jumped into the truck. It was a short trip to Hatvan, and before I knew it we had arrived.

CHAPTER FIVE

The Apartment Complex

Istvan was sure of the address, and after a turn or two we were in front of the apartment on 116 Nagy Street. Istvan went with me to the manager's office and showed him a receipt for the advanced rent payment on the apartment. The manager gave him two keys, and we proceeded to the second floor to apartment 2B.

Istvan unlocked the door and we walked inside. There were two bedrooms, a bath, a small living room, and a kitchenette.

"What was the number of Dr. Torok's apartment?" I asked Istvan in a whisper.

He replied quietly, "4B."

Istvan said, "You remain in the apartment. Peter will park the truck and he and Margit will be upstairs in a few minutes."

Shortly, there was a knock at the door and I prayed that it was Margit and Peter. Istvan opened the door, and to my delight it was them.

Istvan said, " Margit take the room on the left, Peter will sleep on the couch, and

Sandor and I will take the other bedroom."

We all unpacked and put the food that Margit's mother had prepared for us in the refrigerator.

Istvan looked out the window and said, "Peter is back."

He let Peter in and Peter laid the truck keys on the kitchen table.

What time does Dr. Torok return from work?" I asked.

"He usually arrives between 5:30 and 6:00 p.m." Istvan answered. "When we see him coming, I want you to stand outside our door and greet him as he comes up the stairs."

It was 4:30 and I was beginning to get nervous about meeting Dr. Torok.

"Istvan," I said, "I need a bath and I need to wash my clothes. I also need another change of civilian clothing."

"I'll take care of it," he told me and asked Peter to go out and buy some clothes for me.

Peter looked at me as if to measure the size I would wear.

"Whatever fits you should fit me, since we're about the same size," I said.

While waiting for Dr. Tokor to arrive I took a nice long shower.

A few minutes after I dried off Peter came in and handed me a package, which I presumed were my new clothes. I unwrapped the parcel and went into the bedroom to get dressed.

Peter has done himself proud, I thought. Everything fits to a T.

Later I learned that he had purchased them at a flea market that was even better because they were slightly worn and not as noticeable as new ones.

"Are you all ready to eat?" asked Margit.

"I'd rather wait until after I have met with Dr. Torok," I answered.

Peter and Istvan both said they were ready to eat and sat down with Margit and began eating their supper.

At approximately 5:45 Istvan called me to the window and pointed out the doctor to me. He was a short man, about 5 feet 6 inches tall, carrying a black plastic shopping bag.

I immediately went outside our door and waited for him to come up the stairs. As soon as I saw him enter the door I started down the steps.

When he was about three feet from me I said, "Good evening (*Jo estet*)."

"Good evening (*Jo estet*)," he responded.

He went into his apartment and closed the door. I went back up stairs to our apartment after having made contact with him.

Peter asked, "How did the meeting go?"

"I greeted him and he greeted me in return," I answered.

"Margit, could I have something to eat now?" I asked. " I'm starved."

She handed me a plate of food her mother had prepared for us and I ate it.

Istvan and Peter sat down at the table and began to play cards. I had seen my father and his friends play the game they were playing, but I had no idea how to play. They and my father played with a deck of Hungarian cards.

I paced up and down, looked out the window and

every now and then I would watch the card game for a few minutes.

Finally, I said, "I'm tired. I'm going to bed."

I went into the bedroom, crawled into bed, and shortly fell asleep.

CHAPTER SIX
The Grape Festival

I awoke about 7a.m. I proceeded to get dressed and went to the bathroom.

Margit was already awake and in the kitchen preparing breakfast.

"Where did you get the food?" I asked.

"Istvan gave me some money, and I went to the market to shop," she replied.

Soon Peter came, and then Istvan came, and they sat down to eat their breakfast.

"Later we will all walk to town and take part in the local celebration," Istvan informed us. "We need for the town's people to see us on a regular basis and accept us as we move about the city from time to time," he continued.

While Margit was cleaning up after breakfast, we three men sat down at the table, and Istvan gave me some instructions.

He said, "When we go out I don't want you to do much talking and I want you to walk between Peter and me."

I said, "I'll do whatever you think is best."

About 10 o'clock Istvan said, "It's time to go to town!"

The four of us proceeded to walk to town to partake in the celebration of the Grape Festival. At first I was hesitant about being seen too often in Hatvan, but Istvan assured me that if I remained in the apartment people would notice and probably inquire as to why I wasn't at the festival.

I decided I would go with them. It was a short walk to town as our apartment was located on the edge of town.

While walking toward town I noticed the villagers were dressed in their native costumes of Hungary. I also noticed that the factory was in full operation and wondered if the workers would be able to celebrate the festival.

As we were approaching the city, I could hear the music of the gypsy band off in the distance. In a few minutes we were on the edge of a large crowd, who were doing the CSARDAS and thoroughly enjoying themselves. Bunches of grapes were hanging from wires that were strung out across the street. Every once in a while the dancers' would jump up and grab some of the grapes. If the local children caught them, they were taken to a makeshift jail. In order to get out of jail the culprit had to pay a fine and the monies collected went to local charities. Everyone seemed to be enjoying them selves, so I felt that I may as well do the same and I asked Margit to dance with me.

I did the best I could and when we were finished Peter asked, "Where did you learn the Czardas?"

"At the Grape Festival held in my hometown each year," I replied.

After we danced Margit leaned over and kissed me

on the cheek, we walked toward a booth that was selling different Hungarian pastries.

The aroma from the booth prompted Istvan to say, "Let's go over to Nagy's Restaurant for something to eat."

We entered the restaurant and asked for a table for four people. The waiter told us to follow him.

After we were seated and had ordered, a German officer asked the four of us who were seated alongside him and his aide, "What Hungarian wine do you suggest I purchase?"

Captain Franz Mueller was a short, stooped young man. The only thing that looked German about him was his uniform and his blue eyes. He was in charge of security at the Krupp Factory. I had seen Captain Mueller when Istvan and I walked past the Krupp Factory.

"I suggest Tokay wine, as I am sure you would enjoy it," Istvan answered.

The Captain promptly summoned the waiter and asked for a bottle of Tokay.

The table had been set in front of the fireplace. There were plates of homemade breads, pastries, cheeses and thick sausages that had been cooked until their skins burst. Two bottles of wine had also been opened and were setting on the table.

Istvan poured us a glass of red wine, then took a knife and sliced off a piece of sausage and popped it into his mouth. I watched him as he savored the spicy bit of meat before washing it down with a sip of wine.

I fixed myself a plate of bread, sausage and cheese. I wanted to try some wine, but thought I had better not.

I looked at the label on the bottle and it was Egri Bikaver, "Bulls Blood", which was bottled in the town of Eger.

In 1984 when I returned to Hungary I visited the town of Eger and toured the old fort where the Hungarians fought off the invasion of the Turks. It was interesting to see the influence the Turks had on Hungary in their architecture and baths.

Istvan leaned over and said quietly, "Germans are like bananas! They come in bunches. I guess this is for protection."

Istvan said something in Hungarian. I didn't understand him. He could have said, "I'm allergic to aspirin."

CHAPTER SEVEN
Dr. Torok

We finished our meal and decided to go back to the apartment. When we were within fifty or so feet of the apartment, Dr. Torok walked up the street. Istvan gave me a nudge and nodded toward the doctor. When he was abreast of us, I greeted him and he in turn greeted me. The five of us went up the stairs and entered our respective apartments.

When we were inside Margit suggested, "We need to invite the Doctor to dinner."

The three of us quickly agreed that we would invite him for dinner.

Margit said, "I will go over to his apartment and invite him over for dinner tomorrow evening."

"Go ahead," Istvan agreed.

Margit left and I wondered if the Doctor would accept. Istvan and Peter sat down and began playing cards.

Shortly, Margit returned and informed us, "The doctor accepted our invitation. I'll go shopping in the morning to get food to prepare for dinner."

Margit and I watched Peter and Istvan play cards. I still couldn't understand the game and so I ask them to explain. Peter explained the value of the cards to me and how they were playing. It sounded and looked like they were playing a game similar to Rummy.

I soon grew tired, and left the three of them to retire to my room. I couldn't sleep for thinking about Margit. Soon Peter came to bed and in no time he was snoring. I cautiously got out of bed and crept into Margit's room. She was awake and I slid in bed beside her. She was wearing nothing at all and soon we were embracing each other. I left her room about five o'clock and returned to my bed.

I awoke about seven o'clock, cleaned up and went to the kitchen. Peter and Margit were already there and were finishing their breakfast. I sat down at the table and Margit brought me a cup of coffee and some rolls.

When will I ever have fresh orange juice again, I wondered? I had some cheese and salami with my rolls and coffee and asked Margit, "Can you get some eggs when you go to the market?"

"Eggs are available, but they are too expensive, so we only buy them for special occasions," she replied.

"Do you want to go to the market with me?" Margit asked.

"Yes!" I answered.

Istvan looked over at Peter, "You go with them. I'll feel safer if one of us accompanies them at all times."

The three of us left for the market and soon we were shopping for the dinner with Dr. Torok.

When we returned Istvan reminded us, "We will have to go slowly to convince the doctor to leave Hungary. Eventually I will have to tell him who we are and why we are here. I will then show him the letter and pictures of his family. He will then have to trust us if he decides to leave, and trust us to get him into allied hands."

For some reason the hours dragged on. I was getting bored and wanted to get on with my orders to bring the Doctor back. Only time would tell if I was to be successful or not.

Istvan said, "If you are successful in convincing the good doctor to leave with you, the three of us will take you by truck to your destination. We will go north along the Duna (Danube) and cross the river near Vac or Szob. From there you and the doctor will be on your own."

It was almost six o'clock and Dr. Torok had been home for over a half hour.

Istvan asked, "Margit, will you go over to the doctor's apartment and tell him we are ready?"

Margit had done herself well. She had made cabbage rolls and home made bread. Istvan brought out a bottle of wine and set it on the table set for the five of us. Margit left for apartment 4-b.

Shortly she returned with the doctor. We greeted the doctor, and he greeted us in return.

"I would like to thank you for inviting me to dinner," he added.

Margit told each of us where to sit. I would be seated opposite the doctor and next to Peter. Istvan poured the wine for all of us and proposed a toast.

"May the war end soon, and the German's leave as quickly as possible!" he exclaimed.

Margit began putting the food on the table, and soon

we all began to eat. As I said before, Margit did herself proud. The food was delicious.

"Do you have a family?" Peter asked the doctor.

"I have a wife and children. They left for England at the beginning of the war. I was detained because of my engineering background," he replied.

Istvan questioned, "Are you Jewish?"

"Yes," answered the doctor.

Margit asked, "Have you heard that all Jews and Gypsies are being sent to concentration camps?"

He shrugged his shoulders, "I've heard that they were. I'm surely glad my family is not here."

We left it at that and, after small talk we finished our meal. We complimented Margit on the food, and she left us to get us coffee and strudel.

While we were drinking our coffee and eating our pastry, Peter told us about a Jew who was hiding in his hometown.

"I'm seriously thinking of helping him escape to England or Switzerland," he said intently.

There was no comment by our guest, and I wondered if Peter's statement made

an impression on him. Later, I learned that Istvan had put Peter up to tell that story to get the doctor's reaction.

Istvan asked, "Dr. Torok, how long have you been working at the factory?"

"I've been there almost three years," he answered. There were times when I was overworked, suffered humiliation, and wanted to be with my family," he continued.

"What if someone could assure you that arrangements could be made for you to be reunited with your family?" I questioned him.

He seemed to be in deep thought about what I had asked. In what seemed like five minutes, he finally answered my question.

"Yes, I want to be reunited with my family. I have often thought about being able to go to England to be with my wife and children. But how would I be able to do that?" he replied.

Istvan spoke up, "Doctor, this young man here (pointing to me) is an American and his name, like yours, is Sandor. His parents were both born in Hungary and he speaks and understands Hungarian well. Sandor landed under cover of darkness to Esztergom and traveled to Budapest where we met, and we brought him to Hatvan. He has in his possession a letter from your wife and pictures of your family."

The Doctor's eyes widened and his jaws seemed to drop. He opened the package, read the letter and looked at the pictures. His eyes immediately filled with tears.

"How and where did you receive the letter and pictures from my family?" He asked.

"Your wife went to the American Embassy in London and asked them if they would help get you out of Hungary. She explained to them that you were an engineer,
and as far as she knew you were working under duress in a munitions factory," I related to him.

"I was questioned about my family and told what my mission would be. Istvan briefly explained to you how I arrived in Hatvan. Margit is Peter's cousin and she came along to assist us in my mission," I continued.

Istvan asked Torok point blank, "Do you want Sandor to help you rejoin your family?"

Again he seemed deep in thought for a long time, then answered, "Yes, but I am afraid!"

Istvan looked at him intently and replied, "Good, you should be afraid! This way you and Sandor will be really careful in returning safely. The five of us will leave Hatvan next Sunday, since you will not be working that day. Using our truck, we will leave just as soon as it grows dark. You will leave your apartment with your shopping bag, as usual, and nothing else. The four of us will follow you, two at a time. Peter and I will go first, followed by Margit and Sandor. As soon as we start the truck Sandor and Margit will jump in the back. We will try our best to intercept you in front of the Lutheran Church where it seems to be one of the darkest areas in Hatvan. From there we will drive to Aszod, Vacm, Szoband, and then Esztergom. That is where you will have to be really careful. You must cross the Danube by ferry, or if possible by a private boat. Then you must make your way to another crossing point; there Americans who will ferry you across to safety will meet you. From there you'll take a short trip to a British Airfield where you will be flown to Europe and reunited with your family."

Dr. Torok asked, "What is the chance of us being

stopped and questioned?"

"We hope very little, as Sandor made it here without any problems. We know the safest way to cross to the pick up point," Istvan answered.

While the good doctor was taking it all in, my thoughts returned to my first meeting with Captain Adams. Captain Adams told me my mission was classified Top Secret.

"When we finish here," Captain Adams said, "any documents removed from this briefcase are to be returned to it before the case is shut again. The documents are not to be separated. Understood?"

"Yes, Sir!" I replied.

"The details are known in full to you, Bill Donovan of the OSS and me. I want you to read the documents and return them and the briefcase to me. Understood?"

"Yes, Sir!" I replied.

When we had finished, I opened the briefcase and read the contents thoroughly. On completion I did as Captain Adams had ordered.

Dr. Torok brought me back to the present when he asked, "Do you all know that the Germans have been test flying a jet-powered fighter aircraft?"

We shook our heads in disbelief and answered, "No!" in unison.

He continued, "If successful, the jet will be able to inflict losses on the bombers of the Eighth Air Force. The United States must stop production of the engines, and only I know what I have just told you, and nothing else. I must reach England to warn the British and Americans of the Germans' plans to manufacture these engines. You must get me safely back to the allied banks!"

We all agreed that we would do every thing possible to accomplish this mission safely.

Istvan said, "Doctor, you return to your apartment for now, and in the morning report to work as usual. You must continue your work and not arouse any suspicion.

In the mean time we will plan our leaving Hatvan as safely as possible. When you don't show up for work Monday, they will send someone to your apartment to look for you. Then they will question everyone in the apartment building. When they have realized that you have left, all hell will break loose. They will ask the landlord about us, the truck will be mentioned, and then they might have the answer why the four of us were in Hatvan."

"We will have to move fast, but not so fast as to arouse suspicion. It's getting late, let's all get some rest and we will talk again tomorrow evening."

The Doctor left and we all helped Margit clean up the dishes, and we retired to our rooms.

While lying in bed, I wondered what if the Doctor decided to turn us in to the Germans. Finally, with that in mind, I fell asleep.

CHAPTER EIGHT

Preparations for Escape

The next morning I awoke, cleaned up and went to the kitchen to eat the breakfast Margit had prepared.

As I sat down, I asked her, "Do you think the doctor will leave with us Sunday?"

"Yes," she answered, "The doctor wants to be reunited with his family, and he has lost his mother, father, and sister. He has no idea where they are."

"Well" I said, "I guess we'll just have to trust him."

Istvan appeared in the kitchen followed by Peter, who was saying, "I heard the doctor leave for work this morning. Let's hope he carries on as always. After breakfast the four of us will take a ride in the truck and return after dark. This way when we leave Sunday we will not arouse suspicion."

We drove for about two hours and stopped at a family restaurant for dinner. There was a museum in the town, and Istvan felt we should spend a few hours there until it was time to leave for Hatvan.

On the way back to Hatvan we again stopped to eat. When we arrived at our apartment it had already grown dark.

As soon as we entered our apartment there was a knock at the door. I opened it and there stood Dr. Torok. He looked shaken!

"What's the problem?" Margit asked, as she tried to

calm him down.

"I was afraid that something had happened, and you had left me behind," he replied with a shaky voice.

"That was not the case at all. We will not leave you," Istvan tried to assure him.

"We were just trying to set a pattern of being away for a long period of time."

The doctor seemed relieved, "I'm sorry," he said. "I guess I'll return to my apartment."

Istvan told us, "We'd better all go to bed as we are going to get up early, and again leave with the truck, so no one will think anything of the truck not being here Monday morning."

When I awoke early Saturday morning, my three friends were already eating breakfast. I sat down and ate mine and listened to what Istvan had proposed for us that morning.

Istvan told the three of us, "We will leave by truck in a few minutes, and Margit and you will climb into the back, just like you will be doing Sunday."

Margit cleaned the table, washed the dishes, and put them away.

Soon we climbed in the truck and were off to Esztergom, the route we would be taking with Dr. Torok.

We arrived in Esztergom, parked the truck and walked to the pier where the ferry had docked. Peter was wearing a coat and hat belonging to Dr. Torok, and he accompanied me to the ticket office.

"May I have a Sunday departure schedule, please?" I asked.

After I was handed one, Peter and I left for a local café where we were joined by Margit and Istvan.

While we were eating Istvan asked Peter and me, "Did you notice anyone loitering around that might have been members of the Gestapo?"

We both answered, "No!"

"Good! We'll not return until after dark again today. The absence of the truck will hopefully not arouse suspicion when we leave Sunday night."

We returned to Hatvan around 11:00 p.m. and immediately went to our apartment. Dr. Torok opened his door slightly and watched us enter. We retired for the night and I lay awake wondering what was in store for us the next day.

CHAPTER NINE
The Day of Escape

The aroma of Margit's coffee woke me after pretty much a sleepless night. I had a dreadful night lying awake wondering if the Doctor would accompany us.

Would we arrive safely in Esztergom, could we board the ferry without arousing suspicion, and could we travel over land to the river safely? Would my fellow Americans be there to get my signal to come and ferry us back to where we would no longer be in danger?

I got up, dressed and went into the kitchen to eat breakfast.

"We will go into town, do some grocery shopping and walk around as we have usually done each day since we have been in Hatvan. We will purchase some bread and sausage so that we can eat on the way to our destination," Istvan informed us.

Margit said, "I'll remain here in the apartment, make up the beds, and clean up the rooms."

"Be sure and leave everything to make it look like we will be returning and set the table for four," Istvan reminded her.

The three of us left Margit in the apartment. Since it was Sunday there was very little traffic in town, and I was glad there would be little chance of meeting any of the guards from the factory or Captain Mueller.

Peter and I remained outside while Istvan went to

purchase the sausage and bread. In a few minutes he joined us, and we returned to the apartment.

When we arrived Margit had cleaned up the apartment and had set the table for four.

"Peter, you and Margit join me in a game of cards," Istvan requested.

I decided to try and get some sleep, as I knew I would have to be alert for quite some time.

It seemed as though I had just closed my eyes when Peter was shaking me and saying, "Sandor, it's time to leave."

Peter and Istvan left the apartment and shortly Margit and I followed.

The truck was running, and Margit and I quickly climbed into the rear. I knocked on the cab and Istvan pulled away from the apartment building.

We hadn't driven very far when the truck stopped, and I heard Peter greet Dr. Torok. The door closed and we were off on our escape from Hungary.

We drove through Aszad and Vac. A few miles beyond Vac I noticed a thumping noise. I banged on the cab to get Istvan's attention, and he pulled over to the side of the road. Istvan got out and came around the truck.

"We've got a flat tire!" He announced.

"Dr. Torok, climb into the back while Peter and I change the tire," Istvan continued.

While they were changing the tire a truck pulled up, and two German soldiers got out and asked, "What's the problem?"

"We have a flat tire. We would appreciate your helping us fix it," Istvan answered back.

Since there was work involved, they immediately climbed back into their truck and left. Peter and Istvan returned to changing the tire, and soon we were on our way to Szob.

We had been traveling about fifteen minutes when we approached the outskirts of Szob, and in a short time we were through the city to our destination, Esztergom. Szob was less than fifteen miles to the ferry, and I prayed that we wouldn't be delayed so that Dr. Torok and I could make the last trip across the Danube.

Istvan slowed the truck and I knew we were in Esztergom. The truck pulled over, stopped and the Istvan killed the motor. Peter and Istvan came to the back of the truck and lifted the canvas.

"We're here," Istvan proclaimed. "Doctor, I want you to take off your hat and coat and give them to Peter. He and Sandor will go and purchase the tickets for the ferry."

Peter put on the doctor's coat and hat and we left to buy the tickets. It was only a short walk to the office and we had no trouble buying the tickets.

We returned with the tickets and Peter gave the doctor back his coat and hat.

"You've got twenty minutes before the ferry leaves. I suggest we eat a little of the food we brought with us, so you and Dr. Torok can take the rest of it with you," Istvan said.

I said, "Okay, even though I still had the K-rations."

After we had eaten Istvan reported, "It's time for you to go."

We shook hands all around, gave some hugs, said good luck and to be careful.

I hated leaving, as I had trusted my life with the three Hungarians.

CHAPTER TEN
The Final Miles

Doctor Torok and I left and walked toward the ferry. There were a few people on the dock who were also waiting for the ferry to leave. In a few minutes a man in uniform appeared and began collecting tickets. We boarded the ferry, found a seat in the corner and sat down. Soon the ferry began moving and we were headed down the Danube. I closed my eyes and tried to remember the route I had taken to Esztergom. I remembered the barn and part of the road I had taken, but that was all.

I felt the ferry slowing and nudged Dr. Torok and motioned for him to follow me. We were the first ones off the ferry, and I wanted to put the distance between the ferry and the crossing point as quickly as possible. Mileage was no problem, but what we may encounter on our way was our problem. I also had to think about Dr. Torok's physical ability. He was three times my age but later I would learn of his determination to be reunited with his family, would make up for any ineptness.

I had planned to do most of our traveling during the night and resting out of sight during the day.

I wanted to travel as fast as I could and asked the good doctor if he felt up to it.

His answer was, "Yes, I want to get to safety as soon as possible. I'll keep up with you."

We had probably traveled about an hour when I heard a vehicle in the distance. I grabbed Torok by the arm and we ran into the woods and lay down. Two open sedans passed us and the passengers looked like German officers. I wondered if the doctor had been reported missing. He couldn't have, this was Sunday and he wasn't to report to work until Monday. We should still have about eleven hours before he was to report to work. There would be questions and finally a search of his apartment, and questioning the landlord, and a search of all the rooms.

By now Istvan and Peter should be reaching Margit's home. After leaving her they would return to Budapest and leave the truck abandoned. I was counting on them to disappear and hopefully vanish without a trace. It would take days before the truck was discovered and days before the truck and Hatvan were put together.

We returned to the road and once again I picked up our walking pace.

We walked for what I thought had been two hours, and I took the doctor's arm and we sat down on the edge of the road. I lit a match under my coat and dials on my watch showed 1:00 a.m. We had been traveling almost three hours since landing on the shore of the Danube.

I asked, "How are you feeling?"

"Tired, but ready to go," he answered

As we were walking up to the road, we heard the drone of several airplanes coming from the east. I was sure they were allied planes coming to bomb Hungary and soon they would be dropping bombs on a factory in Hatvan.

We began walking again and my plan was to walk another two hours and then rest. Then we would walk until six or six thirty and look for a place to hide until night fell.

When the sun was beginning to rise, I motioned the doctor to follow me. We entered the woods and walked for about a mile until I found an ideal place for us to camp. It was dry and out of the wind and hidden by small bushes and a small dip in the ground.

I gave Dr. Torok a knife, bread, sausage, and some water. I still had my K-rations and chocolate bars. I prayed we would not have to use them.

We had been in the woods about an hour when I looked over and saw that the doctor had fallen asleep. I would soon be joining him.

I awoke, looked at my watch and it showed 11:30. We had slept about five hours. I stood up to try and get the circulation back and motioned for the doctor to do the same.

Off in the distance we could hear vehicles passing, and I was glad that we were off the road.

It was getting late and soon it would be dark. I gathered what few things we had and beckoned the doctor to follow me. I wanted to find the road before it grew dark.

We found the road and waited for the sun to go down.

It was almost dark and the two of us started walking again.

Two hours of walking and ten or fifteen minutes of resting, this went on for quite a while and I had a feeling that this was too easy to be true.

During one of our rest periods I thought about my short stay in the Air Force. We shipped out of Keesler Field for the University of Vermont in Burlington. Here I took my ten hours of pre-flight and attended classes in math, science, weather and other subjects. Just as we completed our training we all received a letter from General Hap Arnold telling us that everyone with previous ground force training were being returned to the 78th Infantry Division in Camp Pickett, Virginia. This was the division I had left to go into the Air Force. They immediately put all of us on KP for three days and we complained.

One day the Company Commander told us to pack, meet in the Orderly Room as we were going back to the Air Force. In no time at all we were ready, loaded up in two and a half ton trucks and we were off. Ten minutes later the trucks stopped, tailgates dropped and we were ordered out. This wasn't an airfield, we were still in Camp Pickett, and now we were assigned to Co. A 264th Combat Engineers, the outfit I would go overseas with.

Spotting the farmhouse where I spent my first night in the owner's barn brought my thoughts back to the present. Now I knew we weren't far from the river where we would make our crossing.

After walking for two more hours I saw the river, and now we must find a place to hide until it grew dark again. At 7:00 p.m. I would go to the riverbank and give the signal for our return. I found a place in a grove of trees and waited for our meeting. At 6:45 we left our hiding place and went to our meeting point. At 7 o'clock sharp I gave the signal with my flashlight. I waited for a return signal, but received none. Every five or ten minutes I would signal again, but no answer. After trying for half an hour or more we left the bank, returning to our hiding place in the grove. We stayed there the remainder of the night.

As we lay in the leaves, I wondered what Dr. Torok must have been thinking. Soon we fell asleep, too tired to worry about tomorrow.

We awoke cold, stiff, and hungry. I gave the doctor one of the K-rations and opened one for myself. I never thought that K-rations would taste that good. My friend seemed to enjoy the meal also. I then gave him one of the chocolate bars.

"I haven't tasted chocolate since 1938," he said.

After finishing our meal we dug a hole and buried the candy wrappers then covered the dirt with leaves. I thought about burning the papers but realized how stupid that would be. Afterwards we sat back and waited for it to get dark

CHAPTER ELEVEN

Discovered

Something woke me! I looked at my watch and it was almost five o'clock. Dr. Torok was asleep and I shook him.

"Be really quiet, someone is moving among the bushes," I whispered.

We crouched down hoping to avoid the trespasser, but he walked straight to where we were hiding.

"What are you doing here?" he asked in German.

I answered in Hungarian, "We are looking for mushrooms."

He couldn't understand me, so I bent down and pushed the leaves away until I found a mushroom and showed it to him.

He didn't seem too impressed and must have wondered what two Hungarians were doing across the river miles from Hungary.

He turned around, took one step, and I found a rock and struck him on the head. He fell to his knees, gasped, and I struck him again and again. When he fell over I knew he was dead.

I panicked but realized we had to hide him before someone else appeared. I picked up what few belongings we had and gave them to Dr. Torok. I grabbed the German under the armpits and dragged him about a hundred yards away. The doctor followed me.

I went back to the scene and spread leaves with a tree branch. Then I returned to the doctor and the German and tried to dig a hole with a stick. It was getting late, so I rolled the German into the small pit I had dug and covered him with leaves. If someone came along they would trip over him.

We hurried to the edge of the forest and waited. At 6:30 p.m. we took off to the river's edge to wait for our rescuers.

While waiting to signal the opposite shore of the Danube, I thought about a boat ride my Uncle Gene took my sister Margaret, cousin Peggy, and me on. We parked my uncle's car in Sayville and rowed across the Great South Bay to Fire Island. In 1938 there was a bad hurricane that hit the coast of Long Island, and you could still see the aftermath of the heavy winds and high water. We fished in the bay and caught a few flounders and some eels. We headed to the island where we would camp out for the night. We cooked the fish we had caught for our supper.

The distance that the doctor and I would travel was about half the distance across the Great South Bay. Right now I would rather be on the bay with my uncle.

CHAPTER TWELVE
Rendezvous

Seven o'clock! I shined my light, and at once I received a response from a light on the opposite shore. In a few minutes I heard the sound of paddles.

"National," I whispered. There was no response.

A few seconds later again I said, but louder this time, "National."

I was answered this time by someone saying, "American!"

I grabbed Dr. Torok and hugged him and explained, "They're American soldiers."

The boat pulled up on shore, two of the rescuers jumped out and helped us both into the boat.

"Take off as fast as you can," I said to the rowers. I have no idea how soon the dead German will be missed!"

The four oarsmen took off as fast as they could, and this time I didn't care how much noise they were making.

What seemed like an eternity was about ten minutes until we reached the opposite shore.

"We're safe now!" I assured the shaking doctor. "You've escaped from your captors in Hungary."

We climbed out of the boat, and one of the GI's got on the radio and asked for jeeps to pick us up. While we were waiting for our transportation, they pulled the boat up and put the paddles in it.

I heard the jeeps approaching and soon two pulled up to where we were standing. The soldiers put the boat on a trailer, lashed it down, and the six of us jumped in and we were off.

CHAPTER THIRTEEN
Debriefing

Thirty minutes later Dr. Torok and I were escorted into General Meade's office where he and Captain Adams were awaiting us.

We walked into the office. I saluted and then introduced Dr. Torok to the two officers.

General Meade shook both our hands and said, "I know both of you are tired, dirty and hungry. We've taken care of all that, and tomorrow morning we will talk and make arrangements for Dr. Torok's flight to England. Follow Captain Adams and he will take care of your needs."

I saluted the general and we followed Captain Adams out. While we were walking to the mess hall, I explained to the doctor what the general had said. He fell to his knees and began crying. Captain Adams stopped, turned around, and waited. He seemed to understand what the doctor had been through, and what was awaiting him in England.

After the doctor had regained his composure, we entered the mess hall. The Mess Sergeant who escorted us to a table welcomed us. It was set for six people; the two of us and the four GI's who brought us back to safety.

Two soldiers who were on KP brought us our food. What a feast! It was the best meal I had eaten since being overseas, T-bone steak with all the trimmings.

Captain Adams sat down with us and over a cup of coffee he asked, "Did you have any problems on your trip?"

"Just a few," I answered. "Like the flares almost catching me just after I landed, vehicles on the highway, convincing the doctor to return with me, the failure to make contact the first night, and killing a German."

"But there were also several people who helped me in my mission. That's what's important and I'm grateful and thankful for them," I continued.

When we had finished eating, Captain Adams told us to follow him. He showed us to a tent where we would spend the night. I looked at my watch and it was almost ten o'clock. We were both tired and ready for some real sleep. We hit the bunks and were soon fast asleep.

I awoke the next morning about eight, and Dr. Torok was already up, showered, dressed, and waiting for me. I jumped up, picked up some clean clothes, and headed toward the shower tent.

When I returned Captain Adams was waiting and announced, "Let's go get some breakfast!"

While we were eating, Captain Adams explained to me their plans to transport Doctor Torok and asked me to relate them to him.

I said to the doctor, "You will be taken to the rear to an airfield where the British will fly you to England."

He had a big smile on his face when I finished.

I wrote my name and home address on a piece of paper and handed it to him saying, "Write me after you are settled in England with your family."

To this day I have never heard from him. Maybe he lost my address, or maybe he was told to never contact me.

CHAPTER FOURTEEN
After the War

Upon my discharge from the Army on April 1, 1946, I returned home and found work in a local pocket book factory until I could enter college under the GI Bill. While reading old copies of THE NEW YORK TIMES, which my father had saved for me, I found the edition of the August 7, 1945 newspaper with the following headlines:

" Reich Escapee, Emerges as Hero in Denial of Nazis Atom's Secret". The story under that by-liner read: "How twice Germany narrowly missed the secret of harnessing the atomic energy by splitting uranium atoms and releasing the most powerful destructive force on earth, was recalled today in War Department reports on the atomic bomb.

Development of the bomb after ten years of experiment and research marks the first time that Professor Albert Einstein's theory of relativity has been put to practical use outside the laboratory. The principal character in the dramatic story of the long search for a method of releasing atomic energy is a physicist, Dr. Sandor Torok, a Hungarian Jew who escaped from the Nazis. He had been working in the Kaiser Wilhelm Institute, which was owned by the Krupp family in Hatvan, Hungary bombarding uranium atoms with neutrons and then submitting the uranium to chemical analysis.

The article continued as to how Dr. Torok escaped and joined his family in England and later migrated to the United States. There was no mention in the article of who aided him or how he escaped as the War Department expressed concern for those living in Hungary who assisted Dr. Torok.

At that time I really didn't care, as I was glad to be home safe and sound. In later years I contacted the CIA, OSS, and the Pentagon for information concerning Dr. Torok. They continually informed me that there were no records of my entering Hungary and convincing Dr. Torok to escape. This is why, over 55 years later, I am writing my recollections of that episode.

In 1983 I returned to Hungary for the second time. This time I paid my own way, (not Uncle Sam). I went to number 16 Garman Street and knocked on the door. A man came to the door and asked, "What can I do for you?"

"Is Mr. Imre Nagy in?" I asked. (That was a fictitious name I had made up)

"No." he replied, "Just my wife and I live here," he continued.

Since he looked to be about in his late thirties, I knew that it wasn't the old lady who had taken me in during the war.

I asked, "How long have you lived here?"

"Ten years," he answered. "I bought this property from and old gentleman who had lived here all his life."

I knew he was wrong about that, but what could I say, the cover up was almost complete. There was no use looking for Peter and Istvan. My next step was to go to Aszod and look for Peter's Uncle and Margit.

When I got back to my hotel I inquired about a train to Aszod. Since there were two railroad stations in Budapest, I was directed to the one I should take.

I rode the trolley to the station and purchased a round trip ticket to Aszod. After a short wait I boarded the train and we were off.

Soon we arrived in Aszod and in no time I was on my way to the farmhouse of Peter's Uncle. As I rounded a turn in the road, I came upon an empty field where the farmhouse and barns once stood. Someone had completed the job of wiping out all traces of Peters relatives. I inquired at the local police station and was told that they had left Aszod over fifty years ago. Now the cover up was complete.

About the Author

Alexander "Al" Feher was born in Manhattan, New York and moved to Ronkonkoma when he was six months old. He attended a four-room school on Long Island and high school in Sayville.

Al entered the Army on March 9, 1943 and was assigned to the 78th Infantry Division in Camp Butner,  North Carolina. After sixteen weeks of basic training, he passed the physical and mental tests to enter the U.S. Air Force cadet training. He was assigned to the 61st CTD at the University of Vermont in Burlington. After completing his ten hours of pre-flight, all Cadets with previous ground force training were released from the program. From Vermont he was shipped to Camp Pickett and assigned to Company A 264th Combat Engineers and shipped overseas to the European Theater.

Upon his discharge, he enrolled in 1946 and began his studies at Concord University. He graduated in 1949 with a BS in Education.

He taught high school for two years in Fayetteville, West Virginia and later accepted a position with United States Steel Corporation in Lynch, Kentucky.

Al is married to the former Mary Jane Minton of Welch, West Virginia. They have two daughters, Janey and Susan.

My Induction Notice

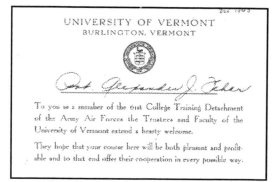

```
                    HEADQUARTERS 311TH INFANTRY
                  Office of the Regimental Commander

                                                     Camp Pickett, Va.

SPECIAL ORDERS )
             :
NUMBER   61  )

    1 thru 29 Extracts.

    30.  The following qualifications in arms of members of this command
for course and arms indicated are announced.

                   HQ CO 1ST BN, 311TH INFANTRY

                   PISTOL, CALIBER .45, COURSE "D"

1.  Thompson, Charlie V.     34371013   Tec 5   Marksman  4 May 44    220
2.  Kilb, Walter E.          12137890   Cpl           "        "      219
3.  Dausch, Harry A.         33374266   Tec 5         "        "      215
4.  Mattucci, Peter V.       13109562   S/Sgt         "        "      215
5.  Falgie, Pasquale (NMI)   33582899   Cpl           "        "      214
6.  Pellet, Richard J.       12157293   Pvt           "        "      207
7.  Layton, Lawrence L.      35116477   Tec 5         "        "      207
8.  retz, Robert J.          16044027   Pvt           "        "      206
9.  Shadlock, John E.        33382126   Pvt           "        "      202
10. Strait, Maurice I.       37343143   Pvt           "        "      200
11. Fishburn, Donald D.      35369267   S/Sgt         "        "      200
12. Hull, Edward J.          32936860   Pfc           "        "      199
13. Weintraub, Samuel (NMI)  32248255   Sgt           "        "      198
14. Rathbun, James F.        37377525   Pvt           "        "      196
15. Feher, Alexander J.      32828755   Pvt           "        "      196


                    By order of Colonel OLMSTEAD:


                                              JOHN V ROWAN, JR
                                              1st Lt Infantry
                                              Adjutant
OFFICIAL:

         MANUEL PALMEIRO
         1st Lt Infantry
         Act'g Pers Off
```

Orders showing where I qualified with the caliber 45 pistol,
hoping I would never have to use it.

UNIVERSITY OF VERMONT
BURLINGTON, VERMONT

To you as a member of the 61st College Training Detachment
of the Army Air Forces the Trustees and Faculty of the
University of Vermont extend a hearty welcome.

They hope that your course here will be both pleasant and profit-
able and to that end offer their cooperation in every possible way.

It took a score of 195 or higher to qualify and only fifteen out
of 120 qualified. This card shows my completion of Air Cadet
program 61st ctd University of Vermont.

```
                  61st AAF College Training Detachment (Aircrew)
                              University of Vermont
                              Burlington, Vermont

353

SUBJECT.  Relief from Air Crew Training

TO      :  All Aviation Trainees from Army Service Forces
           and Army Ground Forces.

The following message to this Headquarters is quoted to all concerned:

"YOU WILL RETURN TO THE GROUND AND SERVICES FORCES ALL ENLISTED MEN WHO
VOLUNTEERED FROM THESE SOURCES AND HAVE BEEN FOUND FULLY QUALIFIED FOR
TRAINING AS PILOTS, BOMBARDIERS AND NAVIGATORS, BUT WHO NOT YET ENTERED
PRE-FLIGHT SCHOOL.  THIS ACTION IS NECESSARY AS A RESULT OF A CRITICAL
AND IMMEDIATE NEED FOR YOUNG, VIGOROUS AND WELL-TRAINED MEN WITL LEADER-
SHIP QUALIFICATIONS TO MEET THE URGENT NEED OF THE GROUND AND SERVICE
FORCES.  IT IS ESSENTIAL TO EVERYONE OF THESE SOLDIERS BE MADE AVAILABLE
FOR PENDING OPERATIONS IN VIEW OF ACCUMULATED SHORTAGES THAT HAVE DEVELOPED
SINCE LAST SELECTIVE SERVICE.  IT IS WITH PROFOUND REGRET THAT I CONSENT TO
DROP FROM THE ARMY AIR FORCES THAT THESE SPIRITED YOUNG MEN WHO ASPIRED TO
JOIN OUR COMBAT CREWS WHICH ARE GAINING FOR US SUPERIORITY IN THE AIR IN
EVERY THEATER OF WARFARE.  IT IS, HOWEVER THE VERY SUCCESS OF THE ARMY
AIR FORCES TEAMS NOW IN COMBAT WHICH MAKES THE SHIFT OF FIGHTING POWER
WISE AND PROPER.  WE MUST PRESENT A BALANCED FRONT TO OUR ENEMIES.  THE
ARMY AIR FORCES TEAM HAS SUCCEEDED BETTER THAN WE DARED HOPE FOR WHEN ARE
QUOTAS WRE SET AND IT NOW PERMITS A REDUCTION IN OUR TRAINING RATE.  WE
AHALL, OF COURSE, CONTINUE TO TRAIN COMBAT CREWS IN AS CLOSE A RATIO AS
POSSIBLE TO OUR EXACT NEEDS.  I AM SURE THAT THESE MEN WILL UNDERSTAND
THAT IN A PROGRAM OF SUCH MAGNITUDE THERE WILL BE TIMES WHEN THE NUMBER
WHO QUALIFY IN ANY PARTICULAR PERIOD WILL EXCEED THE TRAINING QUOTA FOR
THAT PERIOD.  WHILE IT IS MY DUTY TO REGARD THIS MATTER IN A PRACTICAL
LIGHT IT IS MY DESIRE THAT YOU HAND EACH OF THESE MEN AFFORDED, A COPY
OF THIS MESSAGE EXPIANING THE REASONS FOR HIS BEING OBLIGED TO FORGO
THIS TRAINING.  WILL YOU ALSO CONVEY TO EACH MAN MY PERSONAL APPRECIATION
AND THANKS FOR HIS INTEREST IN THE ARMY AIR FORCES AND WISH HIM GOOD
LUCK AND GOOD HUNTING IN THE BRANCJ TO WHICH HE RETURNS.  I AM CONFIDENT
THAT THESE FINE AMERICAN SOLDIERS WHO WANT TO DO THE GREATEST POSSIBLE
DAMAGE TO THE ENEMY WILL PREFER THE OPPORTUNITY FOR AN EARLIER ENGAGE-
MENT TO THE ALTERNATIVE OF WAITING FOR TRAINING WITH THE ARMY AIR FORCES
AT SOME LATER DATE:

                                        HENRY H. ARNOLD,
                                        GENERAL, AAF,
                                        COMMANDING,


                     ALLEN F. ERNST,
                     MAJOR, AIR CORPS,
                     COMMANDING,
```

*Letter from General Hap Arnold to all cadets in Vermont
telling us we want to get back to fight the enemy.*

```
                              HEADQUARTERS
         61st AAF College Training Detachment (aircrew)
                         University of Vermont
                         Burlington, Vermont

SPECIAL ORDERS)
NO.        33)

     1.  The following named Eli, AC, Aviation Students, atchd unasgd to this
det are reld from Aviation Student status and reverted to grades indicated and
are reld from atcho unasgd to 61st AAFCTD(AC), Univ of Vt., Burlington, Vt.
and trfd in grade to Infantry, 78th Infantry Division, Camp Pickett, Va. and
P from this station. /r 17 April 1944 to station indicated rpt upon arrival
to the CO thereat for duty.
     The following men who were accepted for Air Crew trng are hereby reld
from pre-Aviation Cadet status without prejudice for the convenience of the
Government on orders from CG, AAF:
                                  6977355
```

1.1st Sgt. Abued, Mitchell E.,Jr.		2.Sgt Ands, Donald E.	39327190
3.Pfc. Allen, Daniel J., Jr. 32770105		4.T.v. Allen, Don E.	17053462
5.Sgt. Anderson, Jack D., Jr.34955504		6. Apple, William A., Jr.	15302087
7.Cpl. Arnold, John C.	36571387	8.Cpl. Baker, William H.,Jr.	33618573
9. Baran, Theodore J.	37566395	10.Cpl. Barrett, Thomas D.	32753381
11.Cpl. Barron, Joseph J.	36637223	12. Becker, Lloyd J.	35600602
13.Sgt. Bedell, David M.	20271525	14. Redford, Sherman C.	32977133
15.Cpl. Behnke, Edward J.	32083719	16.Cpl. Bell, Claude A.	15314979
17. Bellinger, Daniel E.	36581730	18. Benzel, Robert W.	42020168
19. Bjorkman, Jack L.	39336236	20. Bogdanoff, Nick	39705514
21.Cpl. Brace, James	37509147	22. Brandon, Thomas O., II	11121970
23. Brautigan, Clarence C.	32597682	24. Broughton, Edwin M.	37554126
25.Sgt. Burnett, Adrian O.	34631095	26. Calder, Alexander B.	32811605
27. Cannon, Giles J.	6885461	28.Sgt. Caridad, Louis J.	32158944
29. Carlson, Richard B.	12102869	30. Carter, Beirne B.	13185216
31. Charlton, Ralph G., Jr.	39212877	32. Chesney, Joseph J.	33511709
33. Chew, Billy G.	37529139	34. Cole, John F.	35600438
35.Pfc. Cool, John E.	33560431	36. Cooper, Barton S.	32863335
37.Pfc. Coppage, John F.	37472681	38. Cowan, Douglas K.	39417074
39. Cumming, Harvin M.	39334212	40. Cunningham, John W.	33434200
41. Current, Harry C., Jr.	35805127	42. Cuthill, George H.	35056515
43.Pfc. Davidson, Marion D.	38436992	44. Davis, Carl L.	36660410
45.Sgt. Davison, Charles B.,Jr13076306		46. Deener, William R., Jr.	38512621
47. Denell, John K.	36823612	48.Pfc. Derr, Theodore R.	33371010
49.Pfc. Dings, Gilbert L.	16123640	50. Donckers, Gustave E.	366699-
51. Dragan, George L.	35911711	52. Drynalski, Richard J.	3666930?
53. Dudey, David M.	16102332	54.S/Sgt. Durall, Roy L.	207346?
55. Durivage, Robert J.	15360073	56.S/Sgt. Dymanski, Harold J.35330836	
57. Edwards, Larry E.	37537613	58. Efstration, Paul P.	14192074
59. Ehlert, John F.	37566564	60.Cpl. Ellison, Raleigh W.	33164628
61.Cpl. Emling, Russell J.	36047767	62. Enslie, Robert H.	32941121
63. Everett, Vernon W., J.	31397953	64.Cpl. Falls, Roy E.	38045763
65.Pfc. Feagans, Kester C.	33636048	66. Feher, Alexander J.	32828755
67.Cpl. Fellows, Leslie E.	31190280	68. Fernandes, Anthony	31354809
69. Frasier, Paul L.	34808411	70. Funk, Robert E.	33512542

Orders transferring me and others to
Camp Pickett, 78th Infantry Division.

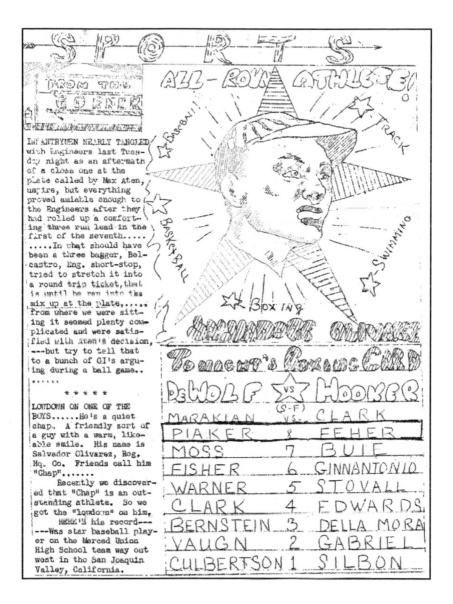

Camp Pickett newspaper showing where I would do anything to get out of KP. Piaker sent me back to KP.

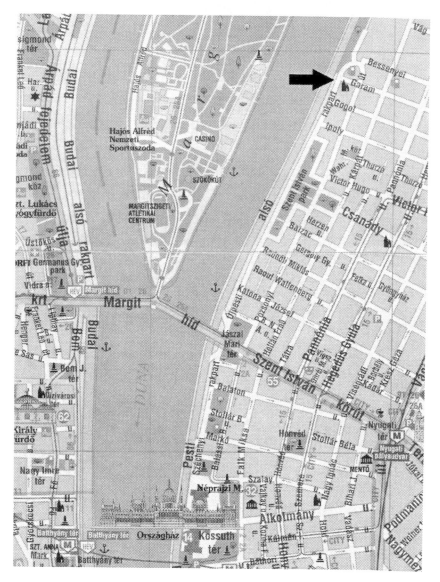

*Garam Street, Budapest. Location of the old lady's house in
Escape From Hungary.*

Additional Copies

Additional copies of *Escape From Hungary*
may be ordered through the author at:

Al Feher
Box 746
Lynch, KY 40855

or online at:

www.westviewpublishing.com

Printed in the United States
147073LV00002B/2/A